50 Premium Sandwich Dinner Recipes

By: Kelly Johnson

Table of Contents

- Classic Philly Cheesesteak
- Wagyu Beef and Truffle Aioli Sandwich
- Lobster Roll with Garlic Butter
- Smoked Brisket Sandwich with BBQ Sauce
- French Dip with Au Jus
- Cuban Sandwich with Mojo Pork
- Chicken Parmesan Sandwich
- Pulled Pork Sandwich with Slaw
- Nashville Hot Chicken Sandwich
- Turkey and Cranberry Panini
- Monte Cristo Sandwich
- Grilled Cheese with Short Rib
- Blackened Salmon Sandwich with Dill Sauce
- Italian Beef Sandwich with Giardiniera
- Reuben Sandwich with Sauerkraut
- Croque Monsieur with Gruyère Cheese
- Roast Beef and Horseradish Cream Sandwich
- Pesto Chicken Caprese Sandwich
- Meatball Sub with Marinara and Mozzarella
- Tuna Melt with Aged Cheddar
- Spicy Korean Bulgogi Steak Sandwich
- Banh Mi with Lemongrass Pork
- Shrimp Po' Boy with Cajun Mayo
- Porchetta Sandwich with Salsa Verde
- Smoked Turkey and Brie Croissant Sandwich
- BBQ Jackfruit Sandwich (Vegan)
- Pastrami on Rye with Mustard
- Classic BLT with Avocado
- Italian Sub with Salami, Capicola, and Provolone
- Crispy Duck Confit Sandwich
- Beef Katsu Sando with Tonkatsu Sauce
- Vegetarian Portobello Mushroom and Goat Cheese Sandwich
- Roast Lamb Sandwich with Tzatziki
- Fried Green Tomato Sandwich with Remoulade
- Eggplant Parmesan Sandwich

- Chorizo and Manchego Cheese Sandwich
- Open-Faced Smoked Salmon Sandwich with Dill Cream Cheese
- Texas-Style Smoked Sausage Sandwich
- Slow-Cooked Barbacoa Beef Sandwich
- Poached Lobster and Caviar Brioche Roll
- Grilled Halloumi and Roasted Red Pepper Sandwich
- Crab Cake Sandwich with Spicy Mayo
- Korean Fried Chicken Sandwich with Kimchi Slaw
- Buffalo Chicken Sandwich with Blue Cheese Dressing
- Honey Mustard Glazed Ham and Swiss Sandwich
- Grilled Pork Chop Sandwich with Apple Slaw
- Steak and Egg Breakfast Sandwich
- Chicken Shawarma Pita with Garlic Sauce
- Spicy Thai Peanut Chicken Sandwich
- Gochujang Marinated Tofu Banh Mi

Classic Philly Cheesesteak

Ingredients:

- 1 lb ribeye steak, thinly sliced
- 1 tbsp olive oil
- 1/2 cup onions, sliced
- 1/2 cup bell peppers, sliced
- 4 slices provolone cheese
- 2 hoagie rolls

Instructions:

1. Sauté onions and peppers in olive oil until soft.
2. Add thinly sliced ribeye and cook until browned.
3. Melt provolone cheese over the steak mixture.
4. Serve on toasted hoagie rolls.

Wagyu Beef and Truffle Aioli Sandwich

Ingredients:

- 2 (6 oz) Wagyu beef patties or thin slices
- 2 brioche buns
- 2 tbsp butter

Truffle Aioli:

- 1/2 cup mayonnaise
- 1 tsp truffle oil
- 1 garlic clove, minced

Instructions:

1. Cook Wagyu beef to medium-rare.
2. Mix truffle aioli ingredients and spread on buns.
3. Assemble and serve.

Lobster Roll with Garlic Butter

Ingredients:

- 1 lb cooked lobster meat
- 4 tbsp butter, melted
- 1 garlic clove, minced
- 2 New England-style split-top buns

Instructions:

1. Mix melted butter and garlic. Toss with lobster.
2. Toast buns and fill with lobster mixture.

Smoked Brisket Sandwich with BBQ Sauce

Ingredients:

- 1 lb smoked brisket, sliced
- 1/2 cup BBQ sauce
- 4 brioche buns

Instructions:

1. Heat brisket with BBQ sauce.
2. Serve on toasted brioche buns.

French Dip with Au Jus

Ingredients:

- 1 lb roast beef, thinly sliced
- 4 hoagie rolls
- 2 cups beef broth
- 1 tbsp Worcestershire sauce

Instructions:

1. Simmer beef broth and Worcestershire for au jus.
2. Serve warm roast beef on hoagie rolls with au jus for dipping.

Cuban Sandwich with Mojo Pork

Ingredients:

- 1 lb mojo-marinated pork, sliced
- 4 Cuban sandwich rolls
- 4 slices Swiss cheese
- 4 slices ham
- 1/4 cup yellow mustard
- 1/4 cup sliced pickles

Instructions:

1. Assemble sandwich layers.
2. Press and grill until golden brown.

Chicken Parmesan Sandwich

Ingredients:

- 2 breaded chicken cutlets
- 1 cup marinara sauce
- 4 slices mozzarella cheese
- 2 hoagie rolls

Instructions:

1. Bake or fry chicken cutlets.
2. Top with marinara and mozzarella, then broil until melted.
3. Serve on toasted hoagie rolls.

Pulled Pork Sandwich with Slaw

Ingredients:

- 1 lb slow-cooked pulled pork
- 1/2 cup BBQ sauce
- 1 cup coleslaw
- 4 brioche buns

Instructions:

1. Mix pulled pork with BBQ sauce.
2. Serve on brioche buns with coleslaw.

Nashville Hot Chicken Sandwich

Ingredients:

- 2 fried chicken breasts
- 1 tbsp cayenne pepper
- 1 tbsp brown sugar
- 4 brioche buns
- 1/4 cup pickles

Instructions:

1. Toss fried chicken in a spicy cayenne sauce.
2. Serve on buns with pickles.

Turkey and Cranberry Panini

Ingredients:

- 8 oz sliced turkey breast
- 4 slices Swiss cheese
- 1/4 cup cranberry sauce
- 2 ciabatta rolls

Instructions:

1. Assemble sandwich layers and grill until golden brown.

Monte Cristo Sandwich

Ingredients:

- 4 slices white or brioche bread
- 4 slices ham
- 4 slices turkey
- 4 slices Swiss cheese
- 2 eggs
- 1/2 cup milk
- 2 tbsp butter
- Powdered sugar, for dusting
- Raspberry jam, for serving

Instructions:

1. Assemble sandwiches with ham, turkey, and Swiss cheese.
2. Whisk eggs and milk. Dip sandwiches into the mixture.
3. Cook in butter over medium heat until golden brown.
4. Dust with powdered sugar and serve with raspberry jam.

Grilled Cheese with Short Rib

Ingredients:

- 1 cup cooked, shredded short rib
- 4 slices sourdough bread
- 4 slices sharp cheddar cheese
- 2 tbsp butter

Instructions:

1. Assemble sandwiches with short rib and cheese.
2. Grill in butter until golden brown.

Blackened Salmon Sandwich with Dill Sauce

Ingredients:

- 2 salmon fillets
- 1 tbsp blackening seasoning
- 2 brioche buns

Dill Sauce:

- 1/2 cup Greek yogurt
- 1 tbsp fresh dill, chopped
- 1 tsp lemon juice

Instructions:

1. Season and sear salmon for **3-4 minutes per side**.
2. Mix dill sauce and spread on buns before assembling.

Italian Beef Sandwich with Giardiniera

Ingredients:

- 1 lb slow-cooked Italian beef, shredded
- 4 hoagie rolls
- 1/2 cup hot giardiniera

Instructions:

1. Pile beef onto toasted rolls.
2. Top with giardiniera and serve with jus for dipping.

Reuben Sandwich with Sauerkraut

Ingredients:

- 4 slices rye bread
- 4 slices corned beef
- 1/2 cup sauerkraut
- 4 slices Swiss cheese
- 1/4 cup Russian dressing

Instructions:

1. Assemble sandwiches and grill in butter until golden.

Croque Monsieur with Gruyère Cheese

Ingredients:

- 4 slices ham
- 4 slices Gruyère cheese
- 4 slices white bread
- 2 tbsp Dijon mustard
- 1/2 cup béchamel sauce

Instructions:

1. Assemble sandwiches and bake at **375°F (190°C) for 10 minutes**.

Roast Beef and Horseradish Cream Sandwich

Ingredients:

- 8 oz roast beef, thinly sliced
- 4 slices sourdough bread

Horseradish Cream:

- 1/4 cup sour cream
- 1 tbsp horseradish
- 1 tsp lemon juice

Instructions:

1. Mix horseradish cream and spread on bread before assembling.

Pesto Chicken Caprese Sandwich

Ingredients:

- 2 grilled chicken breasts
- 4 slices mozzarella
- 2 tbsp pesto
- 4 slices tomato
- 2 ciabatta rolls

Instructions:

1. Grill chicken and assemble with toppings.

Meatball Sub with Marinara and Mozzarella

Ingredients:

- 1 lb cooked meatballs
- 1 cup marinara sauce
- 4 hoagie rolls
- 1 cup shredded mozzarella

Instructions:

1. Simmer meatballs in marinara.
2. Serve in toasted hoagie rolls, topped with mozzarella.

Tuna Melt with Aged Cheddar

Ingredients:

- 1 (6 oz) can tuna, drained
- 2 tbsp mayonnaise
- 1/2 tsp lemon juice
- 4 slices aged cheddar
- 4 slices sourdough bread

Instructions:

1. Mix tuna, mayo, and lemon juice.
2. Assemble sandwiches and grill in butter until golden brown.

Spicy Korean Bulgogi Steak Sandwich

Ingredients:

- 1 lb thinly sliced ribeye steak
- 1/4 cup soy sauce
- 2 tbsp gochujang (Korean chili paste)
- 2 tbsp brown sugar
- 2 tbsp sesame oil
- 2 garlic cloves, minced
- 1 tsp grated ginger
- 2 hoagie rolls
- 1/2 cup kimchi, chopped

Instructions:

1. Marinate steak for **at least 1 hour**.
2. Sear over high heat until caramelized.
3. Serve on toasted hoagie rolls with kimchi.

Banh Mi with Lemongrass Pork

Ingredients:

- 1 lb pork shoulder, thinly sliced
- 2 tbsp fish sauce
- 2 tbsp soy sauce
- 2 tbsp lemongrass, minced
- 1 tbsp honey
- 4 baguette rolls

Toppings:

- 1/2 cup pickled carrots and daikon
- 1/4 cup cilantro leaves
- 1 jalapeño, thinly sliced

Instructions:

1. Marinate pork for **1 hour**.
2. Sear over high heat.
3. Serve on baguette rolls with toppings.

Shrimp Po' Boy with Cajun Mayo

Ingredients:

- 1 lb shrimp, peeled and deveined
- 1/2 cup buttermilk
- 1 cup cornmeal
- 1 tbsp Cajun seasoning
- 4 hoagie rolls

Cajun Mayo:

- 1/2 cup mayonnaise
- 1 tsp hot sauce
- 1 tsp Cajun seasoning

Instructions:

1. Soak shrimp in buttermilk, then coat in cornmeal and fry until golden.
2. Mix Cajun mayo and spread on rolls.
3. Serve shrimp with shredded lettuce and tomato.

Porchetta Sandwich with Salsa Verde

Ingredients:

- 1 lb porchetta, sliced
- 4 ciabatta rolls

Salsa Verde:

- 1/2 cup fresh parsley, chopped
- 1 garlic clove, minced
- 1 tbsp capers
- 2 tbsp olive oil
- 1 tbsp lemon juice

Instructions:

1. Mix salsa verde ingredients.
2. Serve porchetta on ciabatta with salsa verde.

Smoked Turkey and Brie Croissant Sandwich

Ingredients:

- 8 oz smoked turkey breast, sliced
- 4 croissants, halved
- 4 slices Brie cheese
- 2 tbsp cranberry sauce

Instructions:

1. Toast croissants.
2. Assemble with turkey, Brie, and cranberry sauce.

BBQ Jackfruit Sandwich (Vegan)

Ingredients:

- 1 can young green jackfruit, drained
- 1/2 cup BBQ sauce
- 4 burger buns
- 1 cup coleslaw

Instructions:

1. Shred jackfruit and simmer in BBQ sauce for **15 minutes**.
2. Serve on buns with coleslaw.

Pastrami on Rye with Mustard

Ingredients:

- 8 oz pastrami, sliced
- 4 slices rye bread
- 2 tbsp yellow mustard

Instructions:

1. Toast rye bread.
2. Assemble pastrami sandwich with mustard.

Classic BLT with Avocado

Ingredients:

- 4 slices bacon, crispy
- 4 slices sourdough bread
- 4 slices tomato
- 4 lettuce leaves
- 1 avocado, mashed

Instructions:

1. Toast bread.
2. Assemble with bacon, tomato, lettuce, and avocado.

Italian Sub with Salami, Capicola, and Provolone

Ingredients:

- 4 hoagie rolls
- 4 slices salami
- 4 slices capicola
- 4 slices provolone cheese
- 1/4 cup shredded lettuce
- 1/4 cup sliced banana peppers
- 1 tbsp Italian dressing

Instructions:

1. Assemble sub with ingredients and drizzle with dressing.

Crispy Duck Confit Sandwich

Ingredients:

- 1 cup shredded duck confit
- 4 brioche buns
- 1/4 cup caramelized onions
- 2 tbsp Dijon mustard

Instructions:

1. Crisp shredded duck in a pan.
2. Serve on brioche with onions and Dijon mustard.

Beef Katsu Sando with Tonkatsu Sauce

Ingredients:

- 2 (6 oz) beef fillets (ribeye or sirloin)
- Salt and black pepper, to taste
- 1/2 cup flour
- 1 egg, beaten
- 1 cup panko breadcrumbs
- Vegetable oil, for frying
- 4 slices milk bread
- 1/4 cup shredded cabbage

Tonkatsu Sauce:

- 2 tbsp Worcestershire sauce
- 1 tbsp ketchup
- 1 tsp soy sauce
- 1 tsp sugar

Instructions:

1. Season beef with salt and pepper. Dredge in flour, egg, and panko.
2. Deep-fry until golden brown and crispy.
3. Mix tonkatsu sauce ingredients.
4. Assemble sandwich with beef, shredded cabbage, and sauce on toasted milk bread.

Vegetarian Portobello Mushroom and Goat Cheese Sandwich

Ingredients:

- 2 large portobello mushrooms, stems removed
- 2 tbsp olive oil
- 1 tsp balsamic vinegar
- 4 slices sourdough bread
- 4 tbsp goat cheese
- 1/2 cup arugula

Instructions:

1. Brush mushrooms with olive oil and balsamic vinegar, then grill until tender.
2. Spread goat cheese on toasted sourdough.
3. Assemble with mushrooms and arugula.

Roast Lamb Sandwich with Tzatziki

Ingredients:

- 1 lb roasted lamb, thinly sliced
- 4 pita or ciabatta rolls

Tzatziki Sauce:

- 1/2 cup Greek yogurt
- 1/2 cucumber, grated
- 1 garlic clove, minced
- 1 tbsp lemon juice
- 1 tbsp fresh dill, chopped

Instructions:

1. Mix tzatziki sauce ingredients.
2. Serve lamb in pita with tzatziki.

Fried Green Tomato Sandwich with Remoulade

Ingredients:

- 2 green tomatoes, sliced
- 1/2 cup cornmeal
- 1/2 cup flour
- 1 egg, beaten
- 1/2 cup buttermilk
- Vegetable oil, for frying
- 4 slices sourdough bread

Remoulade Sauce:

- 1/4 cup mayonnaise
- 1 tsp Dijon mustard
- 1 tsp hot sauce
- 1 tsp capers, chopped

Instructions:

1. Dredge tomato slices in flour, egg, and cornmeal. Fry until golden.
2. Mix remoulade and spread on bread before assembling.

Eggplant Parmesan Sandwich

Ingredients:

- 1 large eggplant, sliced
- 1/2 cup flour
- 1 egg, beaten
- 1 cup breadcrumbs
- 1 cup marinara sauce
- 4 slices mozzarella
- 4 hoagie rolls

Instructions:

1. Coat eggplant slices in flour, egg, and breadcrumbs. Fry until golden.
2. Assemble with marinara and mozzarella, then broil until cheese melts.

Chorizo and Manchego Cheese Sandwich

Ingredients:

- 2 chorizo sausages, sliced
- 4 slices Manchego cheese
- 4 slices crusty bread
- 1 tbsp olive oil

Instructions:

1. Sauté chorizo until browned.
2. Assemble sandwiches with Manchego and toast in olive oil.

Open-Faced Smoked Salmon Sandwich with Dill Cream Cheese

Ingredients:

- 4 slices rye or pumpernickel bread
- 8 oz smoked salmon

Dill Cream Cheese:

- 1/2 cup cream cheese
- 1 tbsp fresh dill, chopped
- 1 tsp lemon juice

Instructions:

1. Mix cream cheese ingredients.
2. Spread on bread and top with smoked salmon.

Texas-Style Smoked Sausage Sandwich

Ingredients:

- 4 smoked sausages, sliced
- 4 brioche buns
- 1/2 cup BBQ sauce
- 1/2 cup sautéed onions

Instructions:

1. Grill sausages and serve in buns with onions and BBQ sauce.

Slow-Cooked Barbacoa Beef Sandwich

Ingredients:

- 1 lb beef chuck roast
- 1/4 cup chipotle peppers in adobo sauce
- 1/2 cup beef broth
- 1 tsp cumin
- 4 bolillo rolls

Instructions:

1. Slow cook beef with spices and broth for **6-8 hours**.
2. Shred and serve on bolillo rolls.

Poached Lobster and Caviar Brioche Roll

Ingredients:

- 2 lobster tails, poached
- 2 tbsp butter, melted
- 4 brioche rolls
- 1 oz caviar

Instructions:

1. Toss lobster meat in melted butter.
2. Serve in brioche rolls, topped with caviar.

Grilled Halloumi and Roasted Red Pepper Sandwich

Ingredients:

- 4 slices sourdough bread
- 6 oz halloumi cheese, sliced
- 1 roasted red pepper, sliced
- 1 tbsp olive oil
- 1 tbsp pesto
- 1/2 cup arugula

Instructions:

1. Grill halloumi until golden brown.
2. Assemble sandwich with roasted red peppers, pesto, and arugula.
3. Serve on toasted sourdough.

Crab Cake Sandwich with Spicy Mayo

Ingredients:

- 2 crab cakes
- 2 brioche buns

Spicy Mayo:

- 1/2 cup mayonnaise
- 1 tsp hot sauce
- 1 tsp lemon juice

Instructions:

1. Cook crab cakes until golden.
2. Mix spicy mayo and spread on buns.
3. Assemble with crab cakes and lettuce.

Korean Fried Chicken Sandwich with Kimchi Slaw

Ingredients:

- 2 chicken thighs, battered and fried
- 2 brioche buns

Kimchi Slaw:

- 1/2 cup kimchi, chopped
- 1/2 cup shredded cabbage
- 1 tbsp rice vinegar

Instructions:

1. Mix slaw ingredients.
2. Assemble sandwich with fried chicken and slaw.

Buffalo Chicken Sandwich with Blue Cheese Dressing

Ingredients:

- 2 fried chicken breasts
- 1/4 cup buffalo sauce
- 2 brioche buns

Blue Cheese Dressing:

- 1/4 cup blue cheese, crumbled
- 1/2 cup Greek yogurt
- 1 tbsp lemon juice

Instructions:

1. Toss chicken in buffalo sauce.
2. Serve on buns with blue cheese dressing.

Honey Mustard Glazed Ham and Swiss Sandwich

Ingredients:

- 8 oz ham, sliced
- 4 slices Swiss cheese
- 4 slices rye bread

Honey Mustard:

- 2 tbsp honey
- 1 tbsp Dijon mustard

Instructions:

1. Mix honey mustard.
2. Assemble sandwich and toast in a pan until golden.

Grilled Pork Chop Sandwich with Apple Slaw

Ingredients:

- 2 boneless pork chops
- 2 ciabatta rolls

Apple Slaw:

- 1/2 cup shredded apple
- 1/2 cup shredded cabbage
- 1 tbsp apple cider vinegar

Instructions:

1. Grill pork chops.
2. Mix slaw and serve on sandwich.

Steak and Egg Breakfast Sandwich

Ingredients:

- 2 (6 oz) steak cuts
- 2 fried eggs
- 2 brioche buns

Instructions:

1. Cook steaks to medium-rare.
2. Fry eggs and serve on buns with steak.

Chicken Shawarma Pita with Garlic Sauce

Ingredients:

- 2 grilled chicken breasts
- 2 pita breads

Garlic Sauce:

- 1/4 cup Greek yogurt
- 2 garlic cloves, minced
- 1 tbsp lemon juice

Instructions:

1. Grill chicken with shawarma spices.
2. Serve in pita with garlic sauce.

Spicy Thai Peanut Chicken Sandwich

Ingredients:

- 2 grilled chicken breasts
- 2 brioche buns

Peanut Sauce:

- 1/4 cup peanut butter
- 1 tbsp soy sauce
- 1 tsp sriracha

Instructions:

1. Grill chicken.
2. Assemble sandwich with peanut sauce.

Gochujang Marinated Tofu Banh Mi

Ingredients:

- 8 oz tofu, sliced
- 1 tbsp gochujang
- 1 baguette

Pickled Veggies:

- 1/2 cup shredded carrots
- 1/2 cup daikon
- 2 tbsp rice vinegar

Instructions:

1. Marinate tofu and grill.
2. Serve on baguette with pickled veggies.

www.ingramcontent.com/pod-product-compliance
Lightning Source LLC
LaVergne TN
LVHW081501060526
838201LV00056BA/2864